Gruesome Animals in the Ground

Alix Wood

WINDMILL BOOKS

New York

Published in 2014 by Windmill Books, An Imprint of Rosen Publishing
29 East 21st Street, New York, NY 10010

Editor: Sara Howell
Designer: Alix Wood
Consultant: Sally Morgan

Photo Credits: Cover, 1, 3, 4, 5, 6, 7 right, 8, 10, 11, 12, 13 bottom, 14, 15, 16, 18, 19 top, 20, 22 top, 23, 24, 25, 26, 27, 28, 29 top © Shutterstock; 8 left © Clive A. Edwards, USDA; 9 top © Karthickbala; 9 bottom © Pstevendactylus; 13 top © Sandstein; 17 top © Belizar/Fotolia; 17 bottom © Dembinsky Photo Ass./FLPA; 19 bottom © Henrik Larsson/Fotolia; 21 © Nachbarnebenan; 22 bottom © Jason Unbound; 29 bottom © Marlin Harms

Library of Congress Cataloging-in-Publication Data

Wood, Alix.
 Gruesome animals in the ground / by Alix Wood.
    pages cm. — (Earth's grossest animals)
 Includes index.
 ISBN 978-1-61533-734-7 (library binding) — ISBN 978-1-61533-785-9 (pbk.) —
 ISBN 978-1-61533-786-6 (6-pack)
1. Burrowing animals—Juvenile literature. 2. Cave animals—Juvenile literature. 3. Soil animals—Juvenile literature. I. Title.
 QL756.15.W66 2014
 591.56'48—dc23
                                                      2012047733

Manufactured in the United States of America

CPSIA Compliance Information: Batch #BS13WM: For Further Information contact Windmill Books, New York, New York at 1-866-4786-0556

Contents

Who's Underground?

Many revolting animals live in dark holes underground. It can be a safe place to have their young. They can find a cooling escape from the burning Sun or a warm place away from the cold of winter.

Some creatures live underground because that is where their food is. This mole and this worm both eat food found underground. The mole obviously eats the worm, and the worm eats the soil itself.

A mole's **saliva** can paralyze earthworms. The moles can store them alive in underground pantries to eat later. Over a thousand worms have been found in one mole larder!

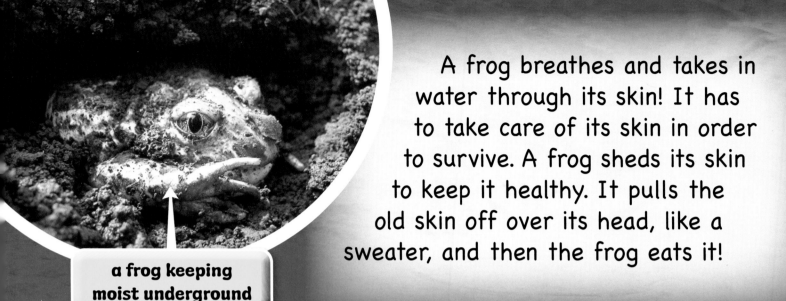

A frog breathes and takes in water through its skin! It has to take care of its skin in order to survive. A frog sheds its skin to keep it healthy. It pulls the old skin off over its head, like a sweater, and then the frog eats it!

a frog keeping moist underground

If an animal lives somewhere cold, it is usually much warmer underground. A female polar bear has her cubs in a den in the snow. In spring they will dig their way out of the den. Their layer of fat helps to keep them warm in winter.

The polar bear is the world's largest land **predator**. Male polar bears can grow to 10 feet (3 m) in length, as long as the height of a one-story building.

5

Wriggly Worms

Worms are pretty gross. They are slimy, wriggly, and don't look very appealing. They are very good for the soil, though.

head end

slime-producing saddle

Under an average football field there are around three million earthworms! To move through the soil, an earthworm eats its way through it. The leftovers pass out as worm-shaped castings. An earthworm produces its own weight in castings every day! It's great for the soil. The Australian giant Gippsland earthworm can grow as big as 10 feet (3 m) long!

If a worm is cut in half, you don't get two worms. Only the head end will live. The worm must have the saddle and at least 10 segments behind the saddle to survive.

a worm cast

A worm doesn't have legs. It is covered in tiny hairs or bristles that help it move. It breathes through its skin, which needs to be moist to absorb **oxygen** from the air. Worms have existed for about 600 million years! Some are so small you would need a microscope to see them. The longest earthworm is the African giant earthworm, which can grow up to 22 feet (6.7 m) long.

Earthworms eat both plants and animals. They don't hunt the animals, they just eat dead ones that they find.

The earthworm's saddle-shaped swollen area secretes a slimy **mucus**. This mucus is also used to form a cocoon to hold the baby worms.

earthworm cocoons

Frogs and Toads

Several frogs and toads like to live in the dark, moist earth. Many will **hibernate** in the soil when winter comes, and some can even survive being frozen solid!

Two frogs that can survive a big freeze are the wood frog and the spring peeper. They both burrow underground or hide under bark in the winter. Sugars in their blood act like **antifreeze** and protect their organs from damage, while the rest of the body freezes solid!

wood frog

These two frogs can survive being repeatedly frozen and thawed through the winter as long as no more than 65 percent of their body water freezes!

Using its balloon-like vocal sac this male spring peeper frog make its high-pitched peeping sound.

The purple frog (right) is also known as the pignose frog. It was only discovered in 2003, as it spends most of its life hiding underground. It comes to the surface for about two weeks a year, in the rainy season, to **mate**. This frog makes a noise like a chicken!

The purple frog's small eyes and large feet for digging are perfect for life underground.

When the Mexican burrowing toad is calling or alarmed, its body becomes inflated.

The Mexican burrowing toad spends most of its life underground. Its back feet have horny, shovel-like growths which help it dig. After a period of rain, it will dig its way out to find a mate. The female will travel up to 1 mile (1.6 km) to find some suitable puddle to lay its eggs. Weather can be very unpredictable, so the toad will mate at any time of the year.

Underground Cities

Some animals dig vast cities under the ground. Rabbits and prairie dogs dig huge burrows which can stretch for miles (km).

Prairie dogs live in large burrows. Their burrows have nurseries, bedrooms, and even bathrooms. They have a special room by the entrance where the prairie dogs can wait and listen for predators before they leave the burrow. They sometimes share their burrows with black-footed ferrets, which hunt prairie dogs!

A prairie dog town found in Texas covered around 25,000 square miles (65,000 sq km)! It was home to about four hundred million prairie dogs.

European rabbits live together in burrows called warrens. Most of the passages are connected and have side pockets where each family lives. There are usually two exits from every area, so if a predator comes in one way, the rabbits can run out through another. The entrances are normally hidden behind a bush or a rock.

a rabbit warren entrance

entrances

rabbit warren

Rabbits mainly eat plants, which are hard to **digest**. Rabbits pass two types of waste, hard droppings and soft, black, sticky pellets. They eat the sticky pellets as they still contain some nutrients. Great recycling!

11

Cave Creatures

In dark caves underground some scary animals find shelter and make their homes. Lions cool off in the heat of the day, and bats hang on the ceiling waiting for night so they can hunt.

Bats hang upside down by their feet when they sleep. When they need to use the bathroom, they hang on with their wing claws and flip their bodies right-side up. They release their waste, and then flip back again! In some caves, the bat droppings pile up as high as 100 feet (30 m)!

Bats find their way in the dark by echolocation. Bats make noises and wait for the sound waves to bounce back off objects. If the noises don't bounce back there is nothing in their way.

Most bats feed on insects, but others eat fruit or fish. Vampire bats feed on blood! They have small, sharp teeth which can pierce the skin without the victim even noticing. Vampire bats can carry and spread the disease rabies.

This vampire bat is biting a cow and drinking its blood.

A vampire bat can only last about two days without a meal of blood. If a bat fails to find food, it may "beg" some from another bat, who will spit up some blood for it to eat!

a grizzly bear

Some big animals like to hide in dark caves. Mountain lions will shelter from the sun in them, and bears use caves to hibernate in. Sometimes a bear will dig a den in the side of a hill, or make a nest under leaves.

Ganging Up

Some underground creatures live in groups called colonies. One ant couldn't kill a mouse by itself, but a thousand of them could!

Several million termites can live together in a colony. Different termites do different tasks in the group. A typical colony has workers, soldiers, and at least one huge egg-laying "queen."

Termites can't digest their own food. Instead, they have tiny **bacteria** living in their gut which digest the wood. The termite eats what the bacteria excrete!

This queen termite can lay around 2,000 eggs a day! She's so big she can't take care of herself. Here, she is being looked after by other termites.

After heavy rain, fire ants make a mound to raise the eggs and **larvae** out of the water zone. Fire ants sometimes kidnap larvae from other nearby fire ant nests!

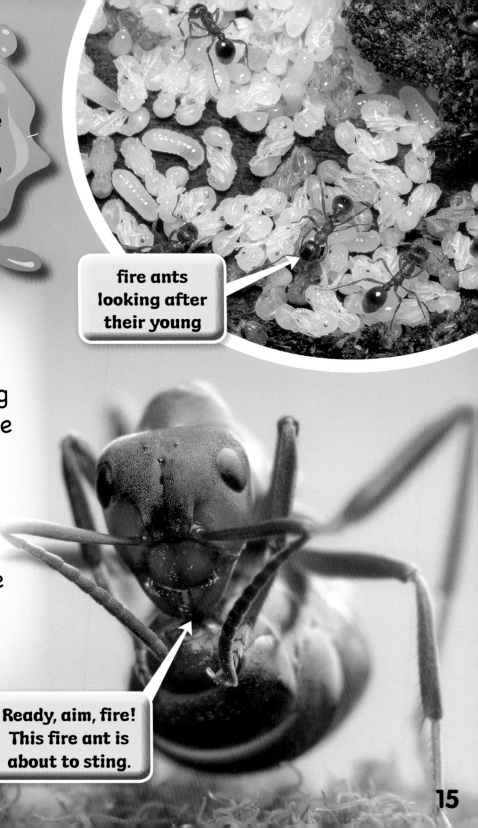

fire ants looking after their young

Many ants bite and inject formic acid into the skin of their **prey**. Stinging ants, like this fire ant, have a **toxic**, **venom**-injecting sting as well. They mainly eat plants but also attack small animals and can kill them. Their sting feels like a burn, which is why they are called fire ants.

Ready, aim, fire! This fire ant is about to sting.

15

Rats and Moles

Rats nest in burrows, or piles of rubbish or timber. They usually sleep in the day and come out at night. Moles can live their whole lives underground.

Rats leave their waste, urine, and hairs wherever they go. They can be infested with human-biting mites and fleas. Rats can cause **allergies** in people, too.

a rat's underground nest

Some types of rat can breed every two to three months and produce 8 to 12 young each time.

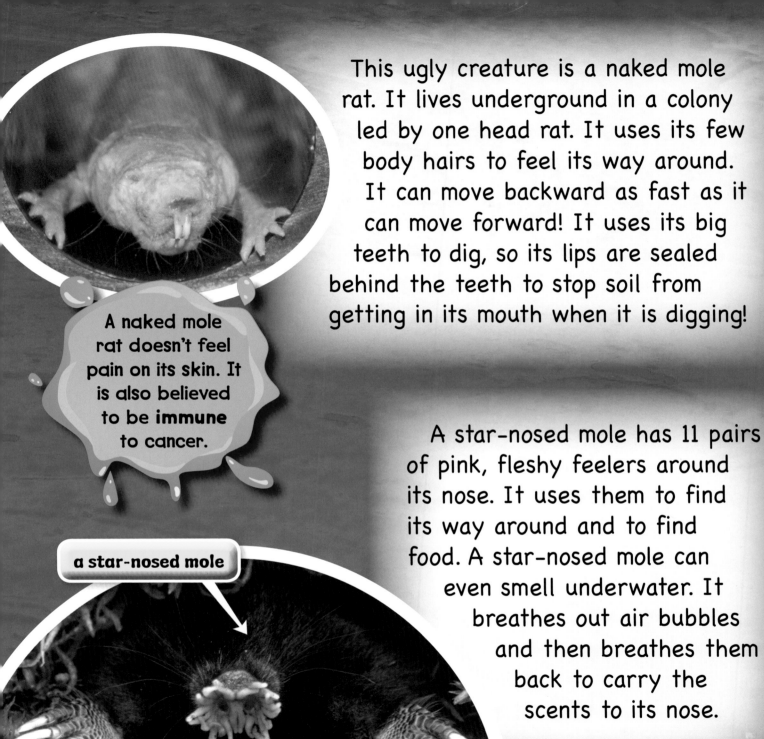

This ugly creature is a naked mole rat. It lives underground in a colony led by one head rat. It uses its few body hairs to feel its way around. It can move backward as fast as it can move forward! It uses its big teeth to dig, so its lips are sealed behind the teeth to stop soil from getting in its mouth when it is digging!

A naked mole rat doesn't feel pain on its skin. It is also believed to be **immune** to cancer.

a star-nosed mole

A star-nosed mole has 11 pairs of pink, fleshy feelers around its nose. It uses them to find its way around and to find food. A star-nosed mole can even smell underwater. It breathes out air bubbles and then breathes them back to carry the scents to its nose.

Underground Insects

Hundreds of insects pass the winter months in soil either as eggs, larvae, or adults. In the spring, most come up into the open air, but some stay underground.

A mole cricket looks a little like half a mole and half a cricket welded together! It has shovel-like legs at the front end, and the back end looks like a cricket. Most species of mole crickets can fly, too. They dig a special horn-shaped burrow in their underground home that acts like a megaphone and amplifies their chirping!

Mole crickets are quite common, but they are hardly ever seen. They are **nocturnal** and spend nearly all their lives in their tunnels under the ground.

A mole cricket has mole-like claws.

Dung beetles love to eat animal waste or "dung." Some dung beetles roll the dung they find into round balls and push it to their underground burrow (right). Others bury the dung wherever they find it. One type of dung beetle doesn't roll it or tunnel under it. They dive right in and live in it! Some beetles lay their eggs in the dung, too, so it is possible for a dung beetle to spend its entire life inside a pile of smelly dung. Gross!

a dung beetle diving in to its home of fresh dung

Most dung beetles search for dung using their sensitive sense of smell. Some smaller beetles just cling on to an animal and wait for them to produce some dung for them!

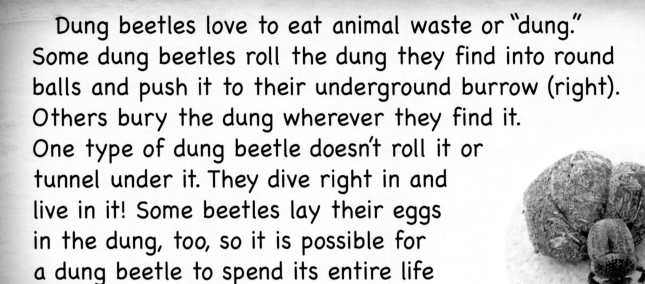

Strange Defenses

It's important to keep your den safe from intruders. Animals have developed a few clever ways to stop anyone from dropping in.

Wombats are great diggers. Their burrows can be from 10 to 100 feet (3 to 30 m) long and up to 11.5 feet (3.5 m) deep. Some are so large that they are visible in satellite images!

Wombats use their rump to block their tunnel. They may use their powerful legs to crush an invading predator against the roof of the tunnel, or drive it off with two-legged kicks.

Wombat burrows are just wide enough for the bulky wombat to fit into.

The pangolin is a great burrower. It can dig up to 8 feet (2.5 m) deep in the ground in four to five minutes. Once it enters the burrow, it blocks the opening.

The pangolin is very weird. Its body is almost completely covered in large scales, like a big pinecone. It has large, powerful front claws for digging, but doesn't use them in defense. Instead, a pangolin curls into a tight ball. It can lash out with its powerful tail, as the sharp edges of the scales can injure an attacker. Sometimes a pangolin will curl into a ball and roll down a slope away from a predator!

A pangolin's last defense from an attacker is to spray a foul smelling, gooey substance from its behind!

a pangolin

Burrowing Crabs

Under any sandy beach there are plenty of creatures hiding. Crabs burst out of their shells and creepy mole crabs burrow under your feet.

When you are paddling in the sea and see strange little "v" shapes made in the water's edge, there are probably hundreds of mole crabs under your feet! A mole crab is actually a type of crab without the claws. Their **antennae** stick out of the sand and form the telltale "V" in the sand.

"v" shapes in the sand

antennae

A mole crab lives buried in the sand at the sea edge. It eats by sticking up its two antennae out of the sand to make a funnel. Tiny food particles collect on their antennae and they put them in their mouths.

a crab shell that has been shed

A ghost crab comes out at night and spends the day in its burrow. When it hibernates in winter, it stores oxygen in air bags near its gills and breathes this oxygen to stay alive! The crab moves sideways at about 10 miles per hour (16 km/h) and can change direction suddenly. Look out!

A crab needs to shed its shell as it gets bigger. It makes a soft shell under the old one, and then the old skeleton cracks along the back and the crab squeezes itself out of it.

A ghost crab's eyes are on stalks and can swivel to give it 360° vision.

Underground Birds

Some birds nest underground. Some use their beaks to burrow into a cliff or the ground. Others move in to burrows made by other animals. It can be a safe place to raise their brood.

Burrowing owls make their nests in anything from an old ground squirrel burrow to a drain pipe. They line their underground nests with animal dung! It is believed the dung makes the nest nice and warm, and attracts insects for the owls to eat. Burrowing owls are especially fond of dung beetles.

a mother burrowing owl and her young

Adult burrowing owls will sometimes capture owlets from other nests and eat them, or feed them to their own young.

Birds called bee-eaters mainly eat flying insects, especially bees and wasps, which are caught in the air. Honeybees are their favorite. They ignore flying insects once they land! Bee-eaters form colonies by nesting in burrows tunneled into the side of sandy banks. You can often spot the entrances by the amount of bird waste streaking the bank.

a bee-eater entering its burrow

Eating a bee can be risky. Before eating it, a bee-eater removes the stinger by hitting and rubbing the insect several times on a hard surface. At the same time it squashes the insect to get most of the venom out.

two bee-eaters arguing over a bee

Crawly Spiders

While most spiders make their home in webs above ground, some spiders will hide in underground burrows instead.

Nearly all tarantulas live underground. Their burrows help them escape the heat during the day. They leave their burrows to hunt at night. To kill their prey they inject it with a **paralyzing** venom using their fangs. Their saliva turns their victim's body into liquid, so that they can suck them up through their straw-like mouthparts!

Tarantulas shed their external skeletons in a process called "molting." They regrow a new one and can also replace internal organs, and even regrow lost limbs.

a tarantula diving into its burrow

The Sydney funnel-web spider makes a funnel-shaped web above ground as a silky entrance to the spider's burrow beneath. It is a venomous spider that can kill humans. Watch out after heavy rain, as they often come out when rain floods their burrows.

a Sydney funnel-web spider

Wolf spiders are large, brown, and have scary, wolflike fangs. Some live in underground burrows. The females carry their eggs on their backs. Once hatched, the baby spiders stay on their mothers' back until they are old enough to take care of themselves.

baby spiders

fangs

Lizards and Reptiles

Many lizards nest underground. Sungazer lizards live in burrows. Their spiny scales are good protection from most predators. Jackals, badgers, and birds of prey hunt these lizards, but getting hold of one isn't easy.

When it senses danger, the sungazer runs into its burrow and shakes its spikey tail as a warning. If a predator grabs the lizard's tail to pull it out of the hole, the lizard puffs its body up with air so that the sharp pointy scales dig into the side of the burrow.

The harder a predator pulls at a sungazer's tail, the tighter the sungazer gets stuck in its tunnel!

Sungazer lizards get their name from their habit of sitting with their nose pointed up at the sky.

Gila monsters spend most of their time underground. They come out to hunt their prey of small mammals and reptiles. A gila monster's bite is venomous. Once the lizard bites, it generally holds on and chews more of the venom into its victim!

The Mexican mole lizard looks like the front end of a lizard stuck on the back end of a worm! It just has two legs, at the front. These forelegs are strong and paddle-like and very good at digging. Long ago it would have had back legs, but now the back leg bones are only visible in X-rays. It is pink, and around 8 inches (20 cm) long. It lives underground in a system of burrows, often under trees.

The mole lizard uses its claws to dig at the front end, and the back end moves through the earth like a worm, using wavelike muscle movements.

a Mexican mole lizard

Glossary

allergies (A-lur-jeez)
Abnormal reactions to substances, often causing sneezing, itching, or rashes.

antennae (an-TEH-nee)
A pair of movable feelers on an insect's head.

antifreeze (AN-tee-freez)
A substance added to a liquid to stop it from freezing.

bacteria (bak-TIR-ee-uh)
Single-celled organisms that can cause chemical effects and diseases.

digest (dy-JEST)
To convert food to be used by the body.

hibernate (HY-bur-nayt)
To pass the winter in a sleeping or resting state.

immune (ih-MYOON)
Having a high degree of resistance to an illness or disease.

larvae (LAHR-vee)
Young wingless forms that hatch from eggs of many insects.

mate (MAYT)
To come together in order to have young.

mucus (MYOO-kus)
A slippery, sticky substance produced by membranes.

nocturnal (nok-TUR-nul)
Active at night.

oxygen (OK-sih-jen)
A colorless, tasteless, odorless gas which forms about 21 percent of the atmosphere.

paralyzing (PER-uh-lyz-ing)
Making powerless or unable to act, function, or move.

predator (PREH-duh-ter)
An animal that lives by killing and eating other animals.

prey (PRAY)
An animal hunted or killed by another animal for food.

saliva (suh-LY-vuh)
A fluid secreted into the mouth by salivary glands.

toxic (TOK-sik)
Of a poisonous substance produced by a living organism that is poisonous to other organisms.

venom (VEH-num)
A poison.

WEBSITES
For web resources related to the subject of this book, go to:
www.windmillbooks.com/weblinks and select this book's title.

Read More

Ganeri, Anita. *Tarantula*. Day in the Life: Rain Forest Animals. Chicago: Heinemann-Raintree, 2011.

Marsh, Laura. *Lizards*. National Geographic Readers. Des Moines, IA: National Geographic Children's Books, 2012.

Rockwood, Leigh. *Worms are Gross!*. Creepy Crawlies. New York: PowerKids Press, 2011.

Index